For my little explorers:
Fynn, Kellen, & Declan

ISBN: 979-8-9882408-1-5

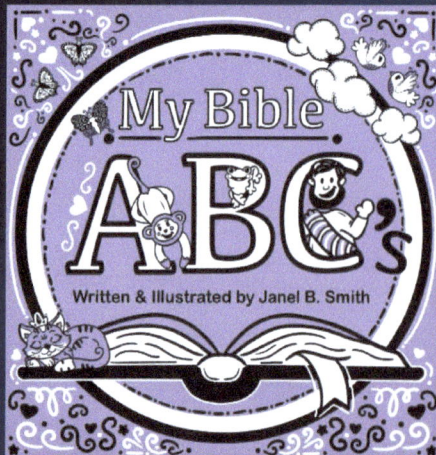

My Bible ABC's

Written & Illustrated by Janel B. Smith

More by Janel Smith

GOD MADE THE GALAXY & ME

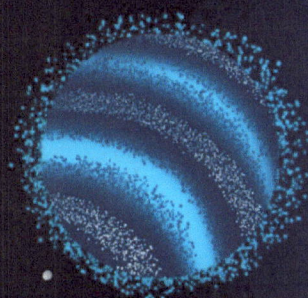

Written and Illustrated
by Janel B. Smith

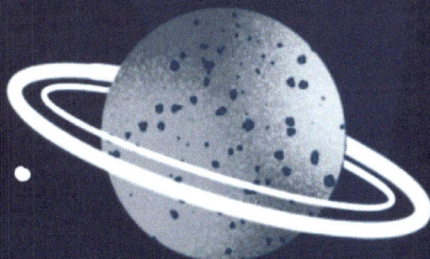

Come with us on a galactic trip.
Climb aboard our rocket ship!

We will witness God's creation, through His handiwork of our solar system.

 **VENUS**

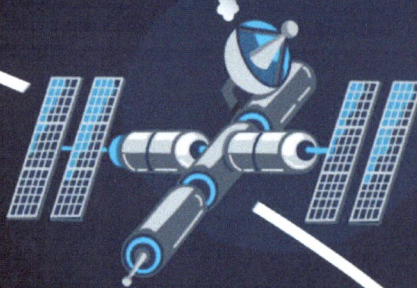

 **MARS**

Let's zoom through the
Milky Way,
the galaxy we call home.

SUN

 **MERCURY**

 **EARTH**

It has eight cool
planets to visit, to
explore, and to roam.

SATURN

With billions of stars, and the sun at our center...

this is where we start our cosmic adventure.

NEPTUNE

JUPITER

URANUS

1 Chronicles 29:11

The SUN

God made our sun with temperatures so high,
At 27 million degrees, it lights up Earth's sky!
Yet, when His love shines through you and me,
His glory burns brighter for all to see!

Matthew
17:20

MERCURY

Mercury, the smallest planet, needs 88 days to orbit the sun.

It's tiny, but mighty, just like you little one!
Even with a little faith, there's nothing God can't do!
Put your trust in Him, and He will see you through.

VENUS

Matthew 5:15

Lonely little Venus, it doesn't have a moon. But this planet doesn't wallow in its gloom.

Be just like Venus, don't hide your light! Be brave, be bold, and don't be afraid to burn bright!

Earth is our home, beautiful and green,
with oceans that wave,
glimmer, and gleam.

But deeper than seas
so wide and blue,
is God's great love, let it
flow through you.

EARTH

Ephesians 2:4

Oh look, the international space station:
a hub for astronauts and experimentation.
Science teaches us about
the planets in space,
God's word teaches us about His
love and grace.

Romans 5:15

MARS

Mars' soil is tough
and its air is cold.
Astronauts who travel
here must be bold.

If something is scary, or a problem gets harder, just be brave little explorer!

Take a deep breath and have no fear. Trust in the Lord, for He is near.

Psalm 143:8

JUPITER

James 1:5

Jupiter is the largest planet in the Milky Way. It spins very fast: twice in just one day.

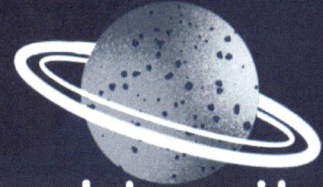

Speed has its place, but wisdom is best. Be steady in His word, and you will be blessed.

Saturn is famous for its icy
rings that shimmer.
It's a dazzling planet, which
fills us full of wonder!

Yet even more amazing than
this planet so divine,
is we are created in God's
image, by His perfect design!

SATURN

Genesis 1:27

Uranus is a planet full of mystery, with supersonic winds and icy debris.

When life gets windy and tries to blow you away, hold tight to Jesus, and He will guide the way!

Ephesians 4:14

Neptune is a planet made of ice and hydrogen.
It's far away from the Earth and sun.

No matter how far through the galaxy you roam, God will be with you, you are never alone!

NEPTUNE

Hebrews 13:5

We've seen a lot of of God's creation: the sun, eight planets, and even a space station.

And while it's time to go,
our journey almost over...
Just remember His greatest
masterpiece is you,
little explorer!

DID YOU KNOW?

SUN

The sun's energy is made through nuclear fusion: hydrogen atoms fuse into helium, releasing immense amounts of energy.

MERCURY

Mercury has a very thin atmosphere or "exosphere" composed of gases like oxygen, sodium, and helium.

VENUS

Venus is often called the "morning star" or "evening star" because it is one of the brightest objects in the night sky, after the Sun and Moon.

EARTH

Over 70% of earth's surface is covered in water, with two percent being made up of glaciers.

MARS

Mars has weaker gravity than Earth, so you would weigh less and be able to jump higher there. It also has two moons!

JUPITER

Jupiter has the strongest magnetic field in the solar system, as well as 95 moons!

NEPTUNE

Neptune has a complex ring system, which is made up of ice particles and debris.

SATURN

Saturn is about 9.5 times farther from the Sun than Earth and takes 29.5 Earth years to orbit the Sun.

URANUS

- Uranus is known as an "ice giant." It is the third largest planet in our Galaxy.

www.ingramcontent.com/pod-product-compliance
Lightning Source LLC
LaVergne TN
LVHW072058070426
835508LV00002B/157